Unique
NEW ZEALAND

Tourists looking down into Deep Cove on the South Island's rugged south western corner in Fiordland National Park.

Silica terraces in Waimangu Thermal
Park, near Rotorua.

NEXT PAGE: Surfcasting on the Taranaki coast.

First published 1994 by
J.M. McGregor Pty Ltd.
P.O. Box 28-309, Remuera, Auckland,
New Zealand.
P.O. Box 6990, Gold Coast Mail
Centre, Queensland 4217, Australia.
© 1994 - individual photographers
and J.M. McGregor Pty Ltd.

ISBN 0 85921 188 6

Designed by Anna Warren
Printed by South China Printing
Company, Hong Kong.

Unique
NEW ZEALAND

McGregor
PUBLISHERS

Inhabited later than probably any major land mass on earth, New Zealand was originally part of Gondwanaland situated on the fault of the Pacific rim. As a consequence it has been subjected to millions of years of earthquakes, eruptions and changing earth structure so that now it is a land of towering mountain ranges, fertile green plains, abundantly stocked lakes and rivers, primeval forests, awesome thermal regions, glaciers, fiords and an experience for the traveller of 'the world in one'.

New Zealand was formed many millions of years before the emergence of most predators so that it lacked native mammals. This allowed the development of flightless birds such as the notornis, weka and the national symbol, the kiwi as well as the huge but now extinct moa. Trees, plants, birds and insects developed in the temperate climate in thousands of varieties found nowhere else.

To this land some 1,200 years ago came the Maoris from Polynesia, finding its resources of food and shelter suited to their lifestyle. Here they flourished until the arrival of Europeans, whose diseases, sophistication and arrogance almost decimated the Maori. More enlightened times have seen the Maori population almost triple in the last fifty years and a real attempt being made to accommodate the demands of both races. It can be said that race relations are probably better in New Zealand than any other country.

Measuring 1,600 km from Cape Reinga in the north to Stewart Island in the south, none of its 3.4 million residents is more than 200 km from the sea and all are close to lakes and rivers.

An economy traditionally based on meat, wool (it has in excess of 60 million sheep), dairying and forestry is rapidly adding a strong export manufacturing base.

To the Maori and European population has been added tens of thousands of Pacific Islanders and latterly a large proportion from the Orient. An active and sensible immigration policy has produced an extraordinary yet harmonious racial mix.

The success of New Zealanders worldwide in the fields of science, business, sport and the arts makes it a respected nation, holding its own against all comers and through it all has emerged a resourceful, talented population, albeit with a ready inclination to assist a visitor — a population of mannered people.

Cape Reinga — the most northern tip of
the North Island.

With its 144 islands and world renowned game fishing waters, the site of New Zealand's first capital, the Bay of Islands is aptly known as 'blue paradise'.

The beautiful Whare Ranunga of the
Waitangi National Trust, Waitangi,
Northland.

Auckland harbour beach in summer.
New Zealand's climate is temperate and
nowhere more so than in the Auckland
and North Auckland provinces.

Auckland's annual Round the Bays fun-run attracts up to 70,000 entries, the biggest event of its kind in the world — some serious, most simply there for the fun.

Auckland city from the air. The harbour
bridge (right foreground) links the northern
suburbs to the city.

Marakopa Falls, Waikato, near Raglan on the North Island's west coast.

RIGHT: Famous mare Horlicks, winner of the 1989 Japan Cup, amongst many races, and over 4 million dollars in stakes, with foal at Cambridge Stud in the Waikato. New Zealand has a very strong horse racing and breeding industry with 60 racetracks throughout the country for gallopers alone.

FAR RIGHT: Cape Kidnappers, on Hawke's Bay coast near the cities of Napier and Hastings, is the site of an enormous colony of gannets.

A Waka, or Maori war canoe, on
unwarlike duties on the Waikato River.

Maori entertainers performing a traditional
poi dance. Pois are swung sometimes at
bewildering speed but always with grace
and graceful body movements.

LEFT: Lady Knox geyser, in the Waiotapu Thermal Valley between Rotorua and Taupo, plays the most frequently of all.

ABOVE: Lake Taupo is New Zealand's largest lake. It is snow fed from the Tongariro National Park, incorporating the North Island's highest peaks, Ruapehu, Tongariro and Ngauruhoe. Trout fishing enthusiasts from all over the world come to enjoy its waters and the abundantly stocked streams.

23

Mt. Ngauruhoe (2,290 metres) with its steaming crater is the most active of the vulcanoes and eruptions of mud and ash are quite common. Nevertheless, this whole area provides some premier ski-fields for many months of the year.

Starting on the slopes of Mount Tongariro in the centre of the North Island, the Wanganui River threads its way down through beautiful native bush and farmland through the city of Wanganui into the Tasman Sea, providing a challenge to canoe and rafting expeditions.

Sunrise on Mt. Egmont (or Taranaki). This beautifully symmetrical mountain dominates a province on the North Island's east coast noted for its dairying and farm production. New Zealand's quite important oilfield is also situated in and off the coast of Taranaki.

ABOVE: Rhododendron garden in the Manawatu. Dozens of different varieties flourish throughout the country.

New Zealand has now a very large horticultural export industry.

NEXT PAGE: New Zealand's capital city, Wellington, and harbour from Mount Victoria with Oriental Bay in the foreground. Centre right leads to the industrial and dormitory suburbs of the Hutt Valley and on to the Wairarapa.

LEFT: The old Parliament and the new 'bee-hive' buildings at lunchtime in the capital.

ABOVE: Dormitory areas of the pretty city of Nelson at the top of the South Island. Most of New Zealand's hops and tobacco come from this area, together with a large proportion of fruit.

A tranquil Marlborough Sound. An idyllic holiday area renowned for its fishing grounds, this province is becoming famous for production of some of the world's very best wines.

The wonderfully productive Canterbury
plains at Fairlie.

The Avon River meanders through
Christchurch — 'more English than the English'.

Far left: Winter beauty, mid-Canterbury.

Left: The Square, Christchurch, Canterbury, with its cathedral reflecting its early days as a Church of England settlement.

Weather beaten and storm tossed pancake
rocks of Punakaiki, Westland.

Viewed from the West Coast, at 3,754 metres, Mount Cook (Aorangi) is the jewel in the Southern Alps, but only one of 22 peaks in excess of 3,000 metres and 140 over 2,000 metres.

Tasman Glacier, Mount Cook National
Park, the ice of which in parts is over
600 metres deep.

40

Tourists on the terminal moraine of the Fox Glacier.

Climbers in the Southern Alps.

A 'must' for visitors! A thrilling trip onto the snow in the Mount Cook National Park and in and amongst peaks in excess of 3,500 metres — sparkling clean air and simply exhilarating freshness.

OPPOSITE: Silver birches on the shores of
Lake Pukaki, with Southern Alps dominated
by Mt. Cook.

ABOVE: Trout fisherman at Lake Middleton,
Canterbury.

A scene played out many times a year
throughout New Zealand, a stock sale at
Tekapo, Canterbury.

'The devil's marbles' — boulders at Moeraki beach, North Otago. Their origins are obscure but they appear to have been eroded from nearby cliffs.

FAR LEFT: Dunedin city and harbour from the peninsula.

LEFT: Larnach's Castle — an extravagance from the Otago goldmining era of the 1860's and 70's.

FAR RIGHT: Queenstown, Otago.
Probably, with Rotorua, New Zealand's
most visited resort. Beautiful Lake
Wakatipu, accessible skifields in winter,
spectacular mountains, facilities for all
sports or just plain, clean, clear, fresh air
and peace.

RIGHT: Shotover area near Queenstown.

50

Woolshed at Lake Johnson backgrounded
by the Remarkables, near Queenstown.

ABOVE: A regular and spectacular event at A & P shows throughout the country, this woodchopping contest at Lake Hayes, Central Otago, is indicative of the long history of New Zealand's extensive and important timber industry.

NEXT PAGE: New Zealand wines are in great demand in the export market. Vineyards appear in many regions, from this one at Wanaka through to Northland.

53

World renowned Mitre Peak in Milford
Sound, with white heron in foreground. Into
these waters sail cruise ships, including
the QEII.

RIGHT: Russell lupins beside Lake Hawea, Otago.

PREVIOUS PAGE: Some of the most productive land in New Zealand, the lush rolling Southland countryside of the Wairaki Valley and the Takitimu mountains.

ABOVE: Winter feeding deer at Wanaka, Otago. Deer farming has become an extensive operation throughout New Zealand, with exports particularly to Europe.

60

There's fun in the snow apart from skiing.
Rafting race time trials on the
Remarkables near Queenstown.

Oban harbour, Stewart Island. New
Zealand's third island, encompassing
122,000 hectares, off the bottom of the
South Island. Densely bush covered, it
teems with bird life and fishing is its
major industry.

Autumn at Lake Hayes, Otago.

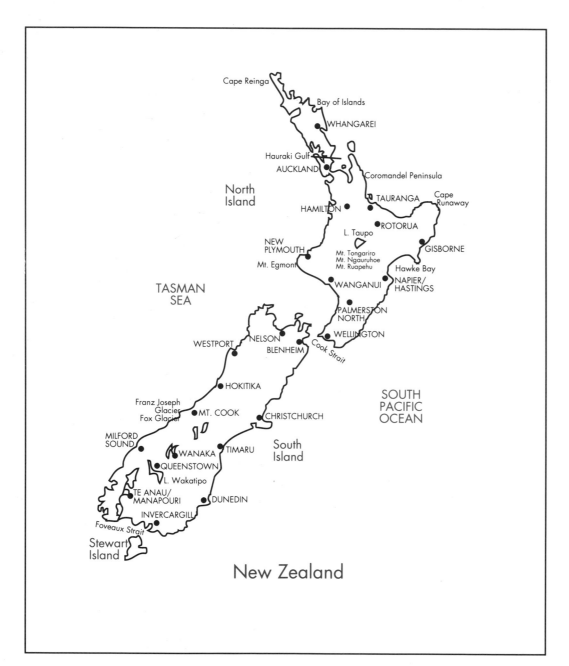

North Island

TASMAN SEA

South Island

SOUTH PACIFIC OCEAN

New Zealand

Cape Reinga
Bay of Islands
WHANGAREI
Hauraki Gulf
AUCKLAND
Coromandel Peninsula
TAURANGA
Cape Runaway
HAMILTON
ROTORUA
L. Taupo
NEW PLYMOUTH
GISBORNE
Mt. Tongariro
Mt. Ngauruhoe
Mt. Ruapehu
Mt. Egmont
Hawke Bay
NAPIER/HASTINGS
WANGANUI
PALMERSTON NORTH
WELLINGTON
WESTPORT
NELSON
BLENHEIM
Cook Strait
HOKITIKA
Franz Joseph Glacier
Fox Glacier
MT. COOK
CHRISTCHURCH
MILFORD SOUND
WANAKA
TIMARU
QUEENSTOWN
L. Wakatipo
TE ANAU/MANAPOURI
DUNEDIN
INVERCARGILL
Foveaux Strait
Stewart Island

64